H.E.R

MW01123964

31 Days of
Healing, Edification and Rest

Nadia Watson-Anthony

Greatness University Publishers
info@greatness-university.com
www.greatness-university.com

ISBN: 978-1-9993481-8-2
ISBN-13: 978-1-9993481-8-2

DEDICATION

I dedicate this book to my mother Charlotte Watson. Thank you for birthing me into the world. Not only did you give me life, you also gave me Christ and without Him I am nothing. Thank you!

I also dedicate this book to Donna K. Lang the woman who spoke a Rhema word into my life. God bless you woman of God.

CONTENTS

ACKNOWLEDGMENTS

I would like to give thanks to the following people that have helped sharpen my womanhood.

Talesiya, Markalen, Isaac, Charles Jr, Kingstyn, Mahoganie, Kayla and Charles II my eight beautiful children. I give all the glory to god for you. Without you coming into my life where would I be? You have all brighten my life. Thank you for being such a great inspiration to me.

I would like to offer a special thank you to Dr. Patrick Businge and his amazing team at Greatness University. I also give thanks to my handsome god fearing husband, Charles Anthony. God answered my prayers and He brought me someone far greater than I could ever imagine in this world. Someone who challenges me grows alongside me and chooses me every single day I live. Because of your obedience, my life seems so much clearer.

Thank you for your love, support and encouragement.

Nadia Watson-Anthony

FOREWORD

Dr Patrick Businge
Bestselling Author, Greatness Researcher
and Founder of Greatness University

FOREWORD

Life is full of challenges that often turn our happiness into sorrow. The American writer Carl Sandburg writes, 'Life is like an onion; you peel it off one layer at a time, and sometimes you weep'. In this transformational book, Nadia Watson-Anthony shares how she navigates the challenges of life on a daily basis. Born and raised in the heart of Fort Worth, Texas, USA, Nadia has not let her challenges characterised by poverty, child pregnancy and abusive relationships become her standard. Instead, she considers her challenges as opportunities for healing, edification and rest. Having gone through life with this mindset, Nadia is now a church minister, marriage counselor, motivational speaker, and life coach.

In this page-turner, Nadia believes that the challenges she has faced are present and often hidden in our homes, workplaces, economies and others spheres of life. She is sure that no one is exempt from these challenges during his or her lifetime. She knows that these challenges are sometimes initiated by the people we love, like and trust. Nadia warns us that when things go wrong, we should not go wrong with them. Like me, Nadia believes that we must refuse to let our struggles, failures and challenges become our standard. Like her Saviour Jesus Christ, Nadia firmly believes that when we face challenges, we need to run to Jesus Christ so that he can heal us, edify us and give us rest. In my personal experience, this requires us to live from a place of faith.

So, if you believe that the solutions to your challenges are found in your faith, then read 'H.E.R Inspiration' and discover the process Nadia is advising you to use from the moment you face challenges to when you witness the healing and are able to live the rest of your life as the best of your life. If you believe as I believe that when the storms of life come your way you need to hold on to your faith, then read 'H.E.R Inspiration' and discover what you need to do to edify your life. If you believe as I believe that there is life beyond failures, then read 'H.E.R Inspiration' and discover how to align circumstances and people to your side so that you achieve unlimited success and find rest in the Lord.

I now have three questions for you: What do you do when you face challenges? What do you do when you are wounded by life? What do you do when life resembles a violent storm? My answer is look at Nadia Watson-Anthony. Nadia is a living answer that there is life after the challenges of life. Nadia's book gives you access to her faith as she navigates through the challenges of poverty, abusive relationships, and teenage pregnancy. Nadia has written this book from her heart to enrich your faith. Read 'H.E.R Inspiration' and discover how to never allow the challenges of life become your standard. If you believe as Nadia that it is not over until you are healed; if you believe as Nadia that it is not over until you are edified; and if you believe as Nadia that it's not over until you rest in the Lord, then read this book for 31 days and witness the transformation in your life.

As you read this book, meditate on the daily reflections. Allow the words therein to move from your head to your heart. Write how you feel in your heart, what you see with your eyes, and what you think in your mind. It is my hope that at the end of this book you will raise above your challenges and confess like St Paul the apostle, 'I can do everything with

Christ who strengthens me'. I now present to you 'H.E.R Inspiration' and may the great faith within you allow you to be healed, edified and find rest.

Dr Patrick Businge
Founder of Greatness University
London, UK, 20th January 2019.

Nadia Watson-Anthony

INTRODUCTION

Nadia Anthony
Church Minister, Marriage Counselor,
and Founder of Christian Maturity for
Teenagers Mentorship Program

Nadia Watson-Anthony

WHY H.E.R. INSPIRATION?

I remember looking all around for God. I will never forget the many of years I struggled with finding my purpose in this life. At this time I had been looking for love in all the wrong places. When I become a mother at a very young age, I felt like my life was over. Little did I know that God would use my pain to create gains. One year, I was experiencing a lot problems that consisted of lack of financial stability, abuse in the relationship, and a lack of support.

At this time, I needed a word from the Lord. I then found myself picking up my Bible and heading to the local park. While in the park, I remember reading scripture. I don't remember which scripture I was reading, but whatever it was, it got me inspired to do the will of God. While reading it, I started pacing back-and-forth yelling out loud, "Yes Lord I will do your will." From that day forward, I made a vow to speak God's word, and that's exactly what currently do. Since then, I have done Bible study, mission trips and speaking engagements. But nothing topped than being able to write my on daily inspiration.

As I continued to develop my spiritual walk with Christ, I found myself creating goals and completing them. This motivated me to inspire other women like me. I let them know that no matter their background or where they were coming from, they could do all things through Christ Jesus.

Today, I find myself becoming more and more confident because of Jesus. Please remember my calling and your calling is unique. Take a minute and think about it. I pray that you all enjoy my inspiration called H.E.R.

Let's get started with HEALING. First and foremost, everyone has a place in their life that has to be healed. The beautiful part of this is that each one of us has a personal savior. In this section of my book, my prayer is that you become open and allow God's word to make you whole. In order to be all God has called you to be, this requires you to be spiritually healthy. If anything is stopping you from your destiny, today will be the day to surrender it all over to Jesus.

Let us now move to EDIFICATION. What do you think of when you hear the word 'edification'? Lately, I have noticed that one of our challenges is understanding what it means to edify one another. In his letter to the Romans 15:2, Paul writs, 'Let each of us please his neighbor for his good, to build him up'. The dictionary defines edification as 'improvement, instruction, or enlightenment'.

Woman of God, we are expected to grow spiritually together. If our knowledge is not increasing and our obedience to God is not continually perfected, we die spiritually. Our Christian life should therefore be about doing the will of God and not just pleasing the flesh. In Christ Jesus, we are new creations. In this edification chapter, I freely wrote whatever God put in my heart. I will therefore help you to be open for change. I will help you be enlighten and transformed.

As you will notice, I will say "obedience is better than sacrifice" after each day. It is my firm belief that it is knowledge and obedience to God that help us determine where our souls will rest for eternity. It is written in 2 Peter 1:5-8 that, 'For this very reason, make every effort to supplement your faith with virtue, and virtue with knowledge, and knowledge with self-control, and self-control with steadfastness and steadfastness with godliness, and godliness with brotherly affection, and brotherly affection with love'. I believe that these are great qualities every Christian needs to have. Again, enjoy this section and allow the Holy Spirit to guide you into all truth concerning every area of your life, and remember to be intentional when dealing with each other.

Finally, once you have been healed and edified, it is time to focus on the last part of this book which is REST. In this chapter the idea of rest is not a secular one but more of a spiritual rest. There have been several times I have found myself relying on people, coffee and motivational speakers to give me peace of mind. It is my prayer that this chapter will inform and challenge you as you search for the answers to your questions so that you resolve the complex issues we are facing in the 21st Century.

- Nadia Anthony

H.E.R. HEALING

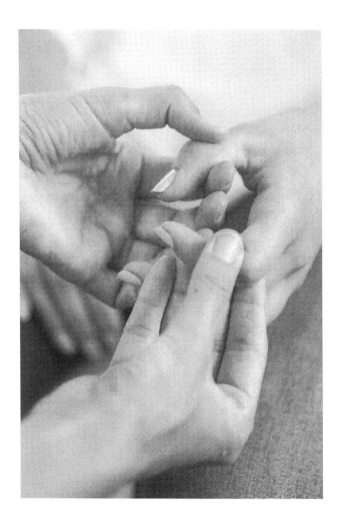

SECTION 1

Healing

In our Christian walk, we should pay more attention to healing. If done well, we will find ourselves gravitating towards God.

Jesus and the twelve approached many people with different ventures in healing so that people would focus more on God. In every parable and story, Jesus would make the main focus on God.

Matthew 4:33 says, "Jesus went about all Galilee, teaching in their synagogues, preaching the gospel and healing all kinds of sickness." For many years, I have seen the miracle power working in my life. I have come to the conclusion that God works in mysterious ways.

I would like to let you know that when you have the Jesus Christ the healer on your side, you will find your true healing. I now invite you to spend ten days reading these biblical verses and reflecting on healing in your life.

Day 1
Matthew 11:28-29

Then Jesus said, "Come to me all of you who are weary and carry heavy burdens, and I will give you rest. Take my yoke upon you. Let me teach you, because I am humble and gentle at heart, and you will find rest for your souls."

Nadia Watson-Anthony

Come

I remember when I was a young girl and I had to fight for everything such as friends and relationships. At this time, I did not quite understand how a God I could not see or touch was going to carry my burdens and give me rest. It was not until I found my place in Christ and decided to obey the gospel of Christ that I began to see life clearly and feel differently.

With Jesus being the answer to all my unanswered question, I knew after following biblical instructions I would be blessed. Matthew 11:28 is where I would start each time a new trail approached me. This scripture made it clear to me that this same God that saved me as a young adult, will continue to walk with me through my entire life and will do the same for you. This is irrespective of what you are currently facing in your life. Always remember that the Lord brings rest to those who obey his word.

Reflection:
Have you obeyed the Gospel?

_____

_____

_____

_____

_____

_____

_____

_____

_____

_____

_____

_____

"Healing does not mean going back to the way things were before, but rather allowing what is now to move us closer to God."

-Ram Dass

Day 2
Psalms 46: 1-2

"God is our refuge and strength, an ever-present help in trouble. Therefore we will not fear, though the earth give way and the mountains fall into the heart of the sea".

From a Christian Woman

Kristi Wilson, Wife, Mother, and Teacher

And we know that in all things God works for the good of those who love him, who have been called according to his purpose.

Romans 8:28

Your Strength

Where is your strength? Where do you run in times of trouble? Who do you call on? This scripture gives life to the lifeless.

Do you remember the time when you thought that the trouble you were facing would never end? I remember it like it was yesterday. For weeks, I felt like I could not escape the worrying in my own head. Somewhere in those lying voices, I had to remember where to run for cover. Somewhere in those lying voices, I had to remember that Christ is my refuge and my strength and with His presence in my life I can face the day like a warriors.

My encouragement to you is that you need to discover ways you can better yourself in spite of any circumstance that comes your way. Today is a new day and you can achieve your goal. One baby step at a time every day can lead to a manifestation of God blessings in your life. With God being your refuge and your strength, prepare to win! I love you woman of God with the love of the Lord.

Reflection
Where is your strength?

_____

_____

_____

_____

_____

_____

_____

_____

_____

_____

Healing takes time. Despite great advances in medicine, the biggest part of your recovery is attributable to the enormous healing power inside you. The body heals itself according to its own timetable--anxious thoughts never hasten recuperation.

Criswell Freeman

Day 3
Psalms 147:3

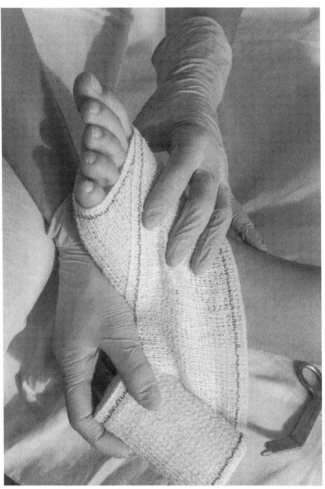

"He heals the brokenhearted and binds up
their wounds."

25

From a Christian Woman

Debbie Tisdale Police Dispatcher

"Do not let your hearts be troubled. You believe in God[a]; believe also in me. My Father's house has many rooms; if that were not so, would I have told you that I am going there to prepare a place for you? And if I go and prepare a place for you, I will come back and take you to be with me that you also may be where I am. You know the way to the place where I am going."

John 14: 1-4

Wounded

Palms 147:3 reminds us that the Lord does hear our cries and heals our wounds. As we deal with daily problems, broken hearts and communication breakdowns, we have to remember that we will become stronger and wiser when we follow the key instruction God has told us to use.

Today, I am holding my 1-month-old son and write my thoughts for you. God never said it would be easy and that is something I have to remind myself daily. On that note, on any place that has been wounded, I urge you to allow the Holy Spirit to heal you on this fantastic day.

Reflection:
What keys are you using to defeat your trailing tribulation?

_____

_____

_____

_____

_____

_____

_____

_____

_____

_____

_____

_____

"Healing is the application of love."
-Iyanla Vanzant

Day 4
Mark 5:34

And he said to her, "Daughter, your faith has made you well; go in peace, and be healed of your disease."

Nadia Watson-Anthony

Your Faith

Mark 5:34, "daughter, your faith has made you well go in peace and be healed of your disease." Instead of focusing on the on physical disease, I would like you to focus more on the concepts of spiritual disease. When dealing with a physical disease, you often think of something attacking your body destroying it until it is no more. That is the same thing when dealing with a spiritual disease. Not only does spiritual disease attack your mind, it also attacks your spirit, your soul and eventually becomes visible and destroys you.

I want to encourage you to read Mark 5:34 where it is written go in peace and be healed of your disease today. Let us go in peace and be healed of anything that come in our way no matter what it looks like. Whether physically or spiritually, we have to remember this scripture and with God loving us, what more can we ask for.

I wish you a blessed day today.

Reflection :
Which spiritual diseases are attacking you ?

_____

_____

_____

_____

_____

_____

_____

_____

_____

_____

_____

"Healing doesn't mean the damage never existed. It means the damage no longer controls our lives."

-Unknown

Day 5
James 5:16

"Therefore, confess your sins to one another and pray for one another, that you may be healed. The prayer of a righteous person has great power as it is working."

From a Christian Woman

Leann Holly, Book keeper

"Consider it pure joy, my brothers and sisters, whenever you face trails of many kinds, because you know that the testing of your faith produces perseverance. Let perseverance finish its work so that you may be mature and complete, not lacking anything."

James 1:2-4

Pray

It is another day to confess our sins to one another ladies. I know there has been a time where you have tried to confide in another woman and it just did not work out. I can go on and on about this topic but you have to find someone who is in God and who will help you out in a time of need.

James 5:16 says that we need to confess our sins to one another and pray for one another so that we may be healed. Indeed, the prayer of the righteous person has great power. Today's prayer focuses more on God bringing righteous people into your life.

I have heard it being said many of times, "I do not need a friend" and "I can pray for myself." The truth is that we all need someone praying on our behalf at all times. If you are a prayer warrior, this is your time to allow the Holy Spirit to work in your life in order to give you guidance on what to do next. Whether this is for you or for a friend let us pray for healing today.

Reflection:
Who is praying for you?
Who are you praying for?

_____

_____

_____

_____

_____

_____

_____

_____

_____

_____

_____

Day 6
Proverbs 4:20-23

"My son, pay attention to what I say; turn your ear to my words. Do not let them out of your sight, keep them within your heart; for they are life to those who find them and health to one's whole body. Above all else, guard your heart, for everything you do flows from it."

Nadia Watson-Anthony

Pay Attention

Day 6 is about being attentive to the word of God. It entails paying attention to our words, listening to our thoughts and reflecting on our actions. This is very hard to do when dealing with negative people in our homes and workplaces.

I would like to encourage you today to put positive things in your ears and before your eyes. This will make things easier for you. Let us be attentive to Gods' word and to His people.

Reflection
What am I paying attention to ?

_____

_____

_____

_____

_____

_____

_____

_____

_____

_____

_____

"I've experienced several different healing methodologies over the years- counseling, self-help seminars, and I've read a lot - but none of them will work unless you really want to heal."

-Lindsay Wagner

Day 7
Jeremiah 17: 14

"O lord, if you heal me, I will be truly healed; If you save me, I will be truly saved. My praises are for you alone!"

Nadia Watson-Anthony

Speak

Did you hear the words of Jeremiah coming right off the pages into your heart? This prayer is the prime example of how we need to speak to God. Sometimes on a bended knees so that we can pour out our hearts to God.

Often, I find myself driving and praying. I find myself walking and praying. However, I rarely get on my knees often to pray to the all mighty God.

Reflection
Which posture do I take while praying?

_____

_____

_____

_____

_____

_____

_____

_____

_____

_____

_____

_____

_____

_____

_____

Day 8
Luke 9:1-2

"When Jesus had called the Twelve together, he gave them power and authority to drive out all demons and to cure diseases, and he sent them out to proclaim the kingdom of God and to heal the sick."

45

Nadia Watson-Anthony

Your Power

Jesus gave the apostle the authority over all demons and sent them out to preach. I am sure he had us in mind.

As the world turn, remember that God has also given you the power to speak to that situation you are facing today. Once again, if you obey, you will win!

Reflection
Which situations are you facing? How are you using God's power to win in life?

_____

_____

_____

_____

_____

_____

_____

_____

_____

_____

_____

_____

_____

_____

Day 9
3 John 2

"Dear friend, I pray that you may enjoy good health and that all may go well with you, even as your soul is getting along well."

49

Nadia Watson-Anthony

Your Words

Wishing you well on this beautiful day. One thing I love about mature Christians is that we don't have a problem with uplifting the flock. Instead of looking at the flesh today, let us look inwardly and bringing about positive words to anyone that comes near. Today is a good day ladies!

Reflection
Which words do you use? Are they positive?

_____

_____

_____

_____

_____

_____

_____

_____

_____

_____

_____

Healing takes courage, and we all have courage, even if we have to dig a little to find it.

-Tori Amos

Day 10
1 John 5:14-15

"And we are confident that he hears us whenever we ask for anything that pleases him. And since we know he hears us when we make our requests, we also know that he will give us what we ask for."

Nadia Watson-Anthony

Be Wise

My dear sister our 10 days of healing have come to an end. I hope you have established confidence in your prayer and developed compassion in your daily life.

I would like to end this section of healing with 1 John 5:14-15. We cannot do anything unless we have the hope and assurance that Christ will back us up fully. In order for us to continually walk in our faith, we must always remember that "obedience is better than sacrifice." You can sacrifice your time, money and even your family but what difference does it make if God has not told you to do that. Instead, be wise and study God's word to seek what God has for your life.

Reflection

EDIFICATION

SECTION 2

Nadia Watson-Anthony

Day 1
1 Timothy 4:16

"Pay close attention to yourself and to your teaching; persevere in these things; for as you do this you will ensure salvation both for yourself and for those who hear you."

Nadia Watson-Anthony

Your Integrity

As Christians, we should have spiritual integrity. As godly women, we should live what we teach. As a godly woman, we should train others in the pattern that we have learned. Our walk should speak louder than our talk.

If we are going to call ourselves Christian women, we should always be placed under Gods control. In the bible Paul always seemed to emphasize on the idea of preaching and teaching. Paul gave specific instructions to Timothy. For instance, in 1 Timothy 4:16, Paul writes, 'Pay close attention to yourself and to your teaching; persevere in these things; for as you do this you will ensure salvation both for yourself and for those who hear you.'

Reflection
Do I walk my talk?

_____

_____

_____

_____

_____

_____

_____

_____

_____

_____

_____

_____

_____

_____

_____

_____

"Obedience is better than sacrifice."

Day 2
Psalm 126:2-3

"Then our mouths were filled with laughter and our tongues with joyful songs. Then the nations said, "The LORD has done spectacular things for them." The LORD has done spectacular things for us. We are overjoyed."

From a Christian Woman

Dana Clair, Human Resources

I can do all things through Christ who strengthens me.

Philippians 4:13

Your Humor

If your home environment is good, peaceful and easy, your life can become peaceful and easier.

Today I wanted to share a little humor with you. Here it is, "And girl don't forget to throw a little Jesus in it," then you really got yourself a winner.

Enjoy the rest of your day and remember to edify someone.

Reflection
Am I humorous? what do I need to improve?

_____

_____

_____

_____

_____

_____

_____

_____

_____

_____

_____

_____

_____

_____

"Obedience is better than sacrifice."

Day 3
Proverbs 31:25-26

"She is clothed with strength and dignity, and she laughs without fear of the future. When she speaks, her words are wise, and she gives instructions with kindness."

Nadia Watson-Anthony

Nadia Watson-Anthony

Sunshine

Good morning sunshine, yes I said sunshine. You are the sunshine. You make Sun Shine every time you step into a room.

Now I can hear some of you saying that Jesus is the light. I must say that you are correct but let me encourage you. If you are doing the will of the Father, you are shining just like him.

Enjoy the rest of your day you ball of sunshine.

Reflection
What happens when you enter a room? Do you make the Sun Shine? Why? Why not?

_____

_____

_____

_____

_____

_____

_____

_____

_____

_____

_____

_____

"We can only appreciate the circle of a sunrise if we have waited in the dark."
-Unknown

Day 4
Proverbs 16:25

One's feelings can be wrong, and not all inner leanings should be heeded. Proverbs 16:25 says, "There is a way that seems right to a man, but its end is the way to death."

Nadia Watson-Anthony

Your Gut Feeling

Have you ever woke up just to feel a gut feeling like something was wrong?

Ladies I am talking about that gut feeling that you just can't put your finger on. That gut feeling that makes you angry. What do you do in those moments? Do you jump to conclusions and start accusing or do you evaluate the situation and seek God?

The edification today is not to trust in your own feelings but allow God and his word to reveal that gut feeling so that you can handle whatever it is according to his will. Remember, a life not surrendered to Jesus is easy prey for Satan's suggestions.

Reflection

How often do you act according to your gut feeling? Have those moments been aligned to God's will? What needs to change in your life?

_____

_____

_____

_____

_____

_____

_____

_____

_____

_____

_____

"Obedience is better than sacrifice."

Day 5
Philippians 4:13

"I can do all things through him who strengthens me."

Nadia Watson-Anthony

Changes

Changes- everybody goes through them. Have you ever woken up and said that I'm fed up! I mean, am I really the only one? It was not until I looked up that I realized how blessed I really was.

Life is always easier to deal with when you have what God has given you.

The edification today is for you my sisters to know that you can do all things through Christ and in Christ. He is your strength! If you want more from God, surrender that situation, that problem or whatever it is that is holding you captive. Give it over to God so that you will be restored.

Reflection
What are you surrendering to God?

_____

_____

_____

_____

_____

_____

_____

_____

_____

_____

_____

_____

_____

_____

_____

"Obedience is better than sacrifice."

Day 6
Titus 2:3-5

"Likewise, teach the older women to be reverent in the way they live, not to be slanderers or addicted to much wine, but to teach what is good. Then they can urge the younger women to love their husbands and children, to be self-controlled and pure, to be busy at home, to be kind, and to be subject to their husbands, so that no one will malign the word of God."

Nadia Watson-Anthony

Be Humble

Edification is even a lot deeper then we think. It can be very refreshing if we give some real thought to it. I took this section to open up so that you can relate to my thoughts. When you think of a younger woman edifying you, how do you feel? Likewise, how do you feel when older woman throw their wisdom in your lap?

For me, it can become intimidating at times. However, one thing I know is that in order for us to grow as women of God, we must remember to keep young friends and older friends in our circle to help and encourage us to remain humble.

Reflection
Am I humble?

_____

_____

_____

_____

_____

_____

_____

_____

_____

_____

_____

_____

_____

_____

_____

_____

"Obedience is better than sacrifice."

Day 7
Philippians 4:19

"And my God will supply every need of yours according to his riches in glory in Christ Jesus."

Nadia Watson-Anthony

Your marriage

Ladies, our edification chapter is almost complete. Not only are we getting great tips on how to be good mothers, daughters, and sisters but we have also received great wisdom that will enrich our marriages.

So instead of focusing on outside influences today, let us focus on our better half and meditate on how God has supplied our needs in this ordained covenant of marriage. Have you ever sat down and asked him how he feels about life? Your relationship? Etc?

Sometime this week, try breakfast in bed ending it with conversation and let us see how far it goes. In this day and time, one thing we can't forget a woman of God is that we still have a duty and that duty is to respect our husbands.

Reflection
How does your husband or partner feel about life? Marriage?

_____

_____

_____

_____

_____

_____

_____

_____

_____

_____

_____

_____

Love bears all things, believes all things, hopes
all things, endures all things."
- *Corinthians*

Day 8
Ephesians 5:21-24

"Submit to one another out of reverence for Christ. Wives, submit to your husbands as to the Lord. For the husband is the head of the wife as Christ is the head of the church, his body, of which he is the Savior. Now as the church submits to Christ, so also wives should submit to their husbands in everything."

Nadia Watson-Anthony

Believe Him

Marriage is a covenant relationship established by our heavenly father. This is a profound mystery that reflects the relationship shared by Christ and His beautiful church.

It is so important to be a great support to your husband because this is so vital for the man. Even though it is hard to understand and explain, God has given us duties as wives. Some of you might be saying, "but I can't commit," "I work a full-time job," "the kids have practice", and "my mother has a doctor appointment." This, I have heard over and over again in my life and the lives of other people. So today remember to edify in submission as purposed by God!

Reflection
How often do you believe or not your husband? What are the effects of this?

_____

_____

_____

_____

_____

_____

_____

_____

_____

_____

When love is lost, do not bow your head in sadness; instead keep your head up high and gaze into heaven for that is where your broken heart has been sent to heal."

- Unknown

Day 9
Romans 8:31-32

"If God is for us who can be against us? He who did not spare His own Son, but gave Him up for us all—how will He not also, along with him, graciously give us all things?"

Nadia Watson-Anthony

Encourage Him

As wives, we are great influences in our husband's life. In fact, God has made us one with our husbands for a greater purpose then we know. Because of this, l firmly believe what we say to them and how we treat them makes a huge difference in how they respond to us.

Nagging at them and accusing them brings worry and makes life harder for them to stay focused. For me, it brought me a lot of sleepless nights and then I finally realized that the way I conduct myself as a wife greatly impacts on how my home functions.

So, if I am doubting, nagging and not trusting, I am just as guilty as anyone else. Today's edification is to remember to love our husbands and speak Gods truth into their life. There is nothing more inspiring to him than to know that God is with working on his beautiful God fearing wife.

Reflection
How do I express my love to my husband?

_____

_____

_____

_____

_____

_____

_____

_____

_____

_____

_____

_____

_____

_____

"Obedience is better than sacrifice."

Day 10
Proverbs 14:1

"The wisest of women builds her house, but folly with her own hands tears it down."

Nadia Watson-Anthony

Desire Him

Desire him. He belongs to you. Ladies this subject is something Christians have a hard time speaking on. " If God gave you that man, what are you afraid of? Why do you lock up when you hear the word SEX? Listen, God made us sexual beings, correct? Did he give us explicit instructions to fulfill these desires within our marriage relationship? Then, what is the problem?

Our husbands need to know that their wives desire them. Today's edification is to follow the scripture. Remember this, love is patient and kind.

Reflection
How do I express my desire to my husband?

_____

_____

_____

_____

_____

_____

_____

_____

_____

_____

_____

_____

_____

_____

"Obedience is better than sacrifice."

REST IN THE LORD

SECTION 3

Nadia Watson-Anthony

Day 1
Psalms 46:10

"Be still, and know that I am God! I will be honored by every nation. I will be honored throughout the world."

Nadia Watson-Anthony

"Peace Be Still"

"Peace be still". I remember hearing this throughout my life. Charlotte Watson says, "Peace be still". Just as much as I heard my mother say these words, I heard God confirming his word too.

This day is moving fast and you may have a lot to do, the one thing I want you to remember is that being still and doing nothing is two different things. When you are told to be still, God wants your time, he wants you to rely on him in all you do. One way or another the Almighty will be praised and honored all throughout the world. Today you have another chance: to give more time to praying!

Reflection
Do I take time to be still?

_____

_____

_____

_____

_____

_____

_____

_____

_____

_____

_____

_____

_____

_____

_____

_____

Day 2
Psalms 55:22

"Give your burdens to the Lord, and he will take care of you. He will not permit your feet to slip and fall."

From a Christian Woman

Pam Pearson, City Administrator

For I know the plans I have for you," declares the Lord, "plans to prosper you and not to harm you, plans to give you hope and a future. Then you will call on me and come and pray to me, and I will listen to you. You will seek me and find me when you seek me with all your heart.

Jeremiah 29:11-13

Your Burdens

When you have a moment look up the word burden. What do you think about when you hear the word burdens? When I first heard this word as a child, immediately I thought it was something that I would receive as an adult. Funny right? You should have heard me as a kid telling my friends "girl I can't wait to get my burdens when I am grown." Well, guess what? I had to be a pretty wise kid because I hit that right on the nail. I received like every other adult my first burden when I was about 21. Only if I knew back then what I know now I would have not carried them by myself.

Psalm 55:22 gives us rest knowing that we have a God that will carry the load and not let us fall even when our feet slip. Today let us focus on resting and unloading our care on Jesus. Charles Anthony often says, "If you are going to pray about it, stop worrying about it." When we are going through something, we need to be real with ourselves and our heavenly father.

Nadia Watson-Anthony

Reflection

Think about your burdens and write them here. Now, take them to the Lord in prayer.

_____

_____

_____

_____

_____

_____

_____

_____

_____

_____

_____

_____

_____

_____

_____

108

Day 3
Psalms 62:8

"O my people, trust in him at all times. Pour out your heart to him, for God is our refuge."

Nadia Watson-Anthony

Your Trust

I love this scripture it is like working out. Once you have a great workout your body will start to relax right after you are complete. Because you have released energy and broken a sweat. It is pretty much the same once you have trusted the Lord and poured out your heart to him. You will begin to feel a release and at that time you will feel God rescuing you, Amen!

When we trust we are placing our confidence in Christ Jesus. When we are delivered and set free, God restores our heart making us new creatures in him. Proverbs 3:7 tells us, be not wise in your own eyes; fear the Lord, and turn away from evil. To trust the Lord is to first fear the Lord. Trusting in God part time is just not good enough.

Reflection
How does your trust in God impact on your life?

_____

_____

_____

_____

_____

_____

_____

_____

_____

_____

_____

_____

_____

_____

_____

Day 4
Isaiah 26:3

"You will keep in perfect peace. All who trust in you, all whose thoughts are fixed on you!"

From a Christian Woman

Carla Oldacre, City Secretary

Trust in the Lord with all your heart and lean not on your own understanding in all your ways submit to him, and he will make your paths straight.

Proverbs 3:5-6

It's Me

Have you ever had a day when you woke up and said, "today is about me?" Maybe you have heard this, "Today I am going to do me boo!" Excuse me if I'm not politically correct but I felt exactly like this today. I had it all planned out in my head. Well, guess what my day didn't go so well. I mean I had it all it planned out; nails, shopping, Starbucks.

Instead I got a flat tire, crying baby, communication breakdown with my husband and teenagers eating everything out of the fridge. And to top it all off, I have a 5-year-old asking for candy, my God! Where are you when I need you? Although, the scripture tells us that we will keep in perfect peace all who trust in God. I am convinced that the way I ended my day had a lot to do with how it started. I started by being selfish, I didn't read my word or make sure my home was in order. Today I want to encourage you to always put God in everything you do. No matter what self tells you, you cannot just do you boo!

You are a vessel being used by God and you will always have a responsibly every day you live. Have a blessed day.

Reflection
What is the place of God in my life?

_____

_____

_____

_____

_____

_____

_____

_____

_____

_____

_____

_____

_____

_____

_____

_____

Day 5
Isaiah 40:31

"But those who trust in the Lord will find new strength. They will soar high on wings like eagles. They will run and not grow weary. They will walk and not faint."

Nadia Watson-Anthony

Run Baby

Good day ladies. I have an aunt that would sing this every Sunday. She would sing it with so much power it stuck in my spirit like glue. "Run baby, you got this." -Susan Clark.

As you move throughout the day remember, those who trust in the Lord will find new strength. Today, you will soar high on wings like eagles. They will run and not grow weary. you will walk and not faint.

Reflection
What are you ready to run for?

_____

_____

_____

_____

_____

_____

_____

_____

_____

_____

_____

_____

_____

_____

_____

_____

_____

Day 6
Jeremiah 17:7, 8

"But blessed are those who trust in the Lord and have made the Lord their hope and confidence."

Nadia Watson-Anthony

Listen

Do you really trust God with the big G or do you trust money? Today let us focus on trust issues. In order to have rest in God, we have to trust him in every area of our lives. I remember walking into a restaurant in 2016 finding coupons scattered all over the floor. At this time I was living from paycheck to paycheck. After bending down to pick the coupons up, I heard the Lord speak to my heart saying that I would receive a blessing unexpectedly from that day forward. Can I testify today?

From that very day, my life has been filled with an abundance of blessings. What would have happened if I did not take the time to listen to the voice of God speak to my heart? Somewhere in this chapter of my life, I found my hope and confidence in the Lord.

Today, I want to encourage you to listen to the small still voice that speaks to your heart. What is it saying to you? If you can't hear it listen a little bit longer and watch God move on your behalf.

Nadia Watson-Anthony

Reflection
Who is in your ears? Which voices are you listening to?

_____

_____

_____

_____

_____

_____

_____

_____

_____

_____

_____

_____

_____

_____

Day 7
Jeremiah 29:11-13

"For I know the plans I have for you," says the Lord. "They are plans for good and not for disaster, to give you a future and a hope."

Nadia Watson-Anthony

Your Suffering

Good morning. Did you read the scripture above? Jeremiah 29:11 makes you think of a security cover. Cleary God has a plan for you so just know that God is good, even though some days are not very clear to you.

Today, I want to encourage you that the suffering we all go through cannot always be explained. If we can remember what God told Jeremiah, we can face anything that comes our way, whether long-term or short - the term we got this.

Reflection
What are you suffering from?
Take it to the Lord in prayer.

_____

_____

_____

_____

_____

_____

_____

_____

_____

_____

_____

_____

_____

_____

Day 8
Matthew 11:28-30

"Come to me, all you who are weary and burdened, and I will give you rest. Take my yoke upon you and learn from me, for I am gentle and humble in heart, and you will find rest for your souls. For my yoke is easy and my burden is light."

129

Nadia Watson-Anthony

Rest

Can you actually believe that there is a place to rest in God. Before work there is noise, when you get in the car you hear a noise. You finally make it to work and all you hear his noise, gossip, and more noise. Sometimes in life, you have to be the leader; maybe you can change the noise by adding your Christian thoughts to the conversation. "Come to me, all you who are weary and burdened, and I will give you rest. Take my yoke upon you and learn from me, for I am gentle and humble in heart, and you will find rest for your souls. For my yoke is easy and my burden is light."

Whatever your circumstance is remember you are not alone and rest is available for you.

Nadia Watson-Anthony

Reflection
Find time to rest. What are the fruits of this?

_____

_____

_____

_____

_____

_____

_____

_____

_____

_____

_____

_____

_____

_____

_____

Day 9
Philippians 4:7

"And the peace of God, which surpasses all understanding, will guard your hearts and your minds in Christ Jesus."

Nadia Watson-Anthony

From a Christian Woman

**Above all else, guard your heart, for everything you do flows from it.
Proverbs 4:23**

Maria Goggans, Municipal Judge

Your Peace

Do you have friends that are outside the body of Christ? I do, and guess what? They deal with their problems differently than I do. As a believer, when you place your full confidence in Jesus you will learn that there is a supernatural peace you will receive. I call it an inner calmness that will take over your heart. Your friends will not be able to fathom that kind of peace.

My encouragement today is helping someone by introducing Bible principles to them. Give someone Christ today.

Reflection
To whom can I introduce the Biblical principles?

_____

_____

_____

_____

_____

_____

_____

_____

_____

_____

_____

_____

_____

_____

_____

Day 10
Hebrew 4:1-3

'Therefore, since the promise of entering his rest still stands, let us be careful that none of you be found to have fallen short of it. For we also have had the good news proclaimed to us, just as they did; but the message they heard was of no value to them, because they did not share the faith of those who obeyed. Now we who have believed enter that rest, just as God has said, "So I declared on oath in my anger, 'They shall never enter my rest.' And yet his works have been finished since the creation of the world."

Nadia Watson-Anthony

Rest in the Lord

My friend we have completed our 10 days. Once again I hope you have grown as much as I have. Before closing out this section, let us talk a bit longer. Did you know rest is one of the greatest gifts that God gave to mankind?

Think about it ladies, when you don't sleep and someone asks you to do something how do you feel? I feel angry, upset and moody, so my physical rest is very important. When it comes to spiritual rest, I believe that it is just as important. As humans, it is our natural ability to associate rest with sleep. Gods rest is profound and deeper than we can imagine when seeking rest always remember ladies or whoever is reading this, that obedience is better than sacrifice. If you obey God you will not sacrifice your soul. Out of obedience comes life and that life is in Christ Jesus.

Reflection
What have you learnt about resting in the Lord?

_____

_____

_____

_____

_____

_____

_____

_____

_____

_____

_____

_____

_____

_____

ABOUT THE AUTHOR

ABOUT THE AUTHOR

Nadia Watson-Anthony is a woman of God, a dedicated wife, mother, and daughter. She has been blessed to graduate from Sunset Bible Institute with an Associate Degree in Biblical Studies. She is currently a student at Amridge University working to receive a Bachelor of Science degree in Business Management, in the year of 2020. She is also a minister of the Gospel, marriage counselor, life coach and founder of Christian Maturity for Teenagers mentorship program. She has been blessed to co-author "Jesus changed our lives" and "Les Brown changed our lives". Feel free to contact Nadia Watson-Anthony at herinspirationbook@gmail.com